INDIA BEFORE THE ENGLISH

Lecture delivered before the
East India Association, London,
April 8th and May 13th, 1897

INDIA BEFORE THE ENGLISH

R. SEWELL

GYAN

Published by

Gyan Publishing House
5, Ansari Road
Daryaganj, New Delhi-110002
Phone: 011-47034999, 9811692060
E-mail: books@gyanbooks.com

Distribution Network
gyanbooks.com
India, USA, Canada, UK, Australia, France

ISBN : 978-81-212-3587-7 (PB)
First Published, 1898

2nd Impression 2020

Printed at: Gyan Press, Delhi.

India Before The English
Author: R. Sewell

CONTENTS.

INDIA BEFORE THE ENGLISH.

INTRODUCTORY.

AMIDST a babel of contending opinions as to the success or non-success of British administration in India, when a large number of disputants maintain that progress in that country has been phenomenal, while others declare that England is ruining India body and soul, it will be well for a few moments to turn from the war of words and clash of conflicting arguments to the solid standpoint of historic truth; and to attempt to gather from unimpeachable ancient records how the matter stands. For I am convinced that in the minds of the majority there is much misty ignorance regarding the true condition of India before the advent of the British, so that opinions are often formed upon bases quite unsound.

The case stands broadly thus: Many Hindus are convinced that their country was better governed by their own rulers than it is now, and some people in this country think the same thing. Well, if that be the case, Her Majesty's Government ought to learn the truth. It would lead to better government in future. And if it is not the case, the Hindus ought to learn the truth. It would lead to their greater contentment in the future; and contentment means happiness. So that for the benefit of both sides investigation can, I think, only lead to good results. But at the outset the enquiry must be conducted on purely historical lines, since it is on those lines alone that we can proceed with safety. We want the actual facts; nothing else is of any value.

The difficulty is how to treat the subject. It would, of course, be impossible to satisfy everyone, even were our historical foothold of the firmest. If I were to take one period only, such a course would naturally be open to objection. If I were to attempt to paint the condition of Southern India 150 years ago it would be argued that such a selection would preclude the possibility of fair judgment, since the country was then in a very chaotic, almost anarchical, condition; while if I were to select solely the government of the Cholas 1,000 years ago, I should lay myself open to the rejoinder that that period is too remote. I do not therefore pretend to take any special period. I merely hope to be able, from contemporary records, in a few odd corners to lift the veil which hides the present from the past, and to throw a little light on some interesting questions of the day.

I desire first to call attention to the fact, insufficiently grasped I think even by English gentlemen long resident in India, that from the earliest times the Hindus have been, as compared with some European nations, a people wanting in the historic faculty—unaccustomed to retrospects; they are therefore by nature unused to the habit that prevails amongst educated Englishmen of comparing what is with what was. They have very few ancient chronicles of contemporaneous events of any historical value; and those few are not studied in a critical spirit. They have no autobiographies, no historical novels, to guide them as to the condition of their country in past days; so that obviously they can form no sound judgment as to whether the government of the English has proved a blessing or a curse to their country. And I think that it would prove of incalculable advantage both to India and England were their own history and the growth of the various peoples and nations taught in the Hindu schools in such a way as to implant in the minds of their young men sound and truthful conceptions of the condition of the country in days before the English acquired the reins of Government.

The Hindus, as well as many Englishmen, are apt to dream of a past golden age, when all India was governed by one Emperor native-born. They talk of the grand days of Râma, of Asoka, of Vikramâditya and others, but I hope to be able to prove that no such empire ever existed. The Hindus think that taxation under native rule was lighter and less harassing than at present. I shall shew from contemporary documents that under one of the purest and most long-lived Hindu sovereignties—that of the Cholas—taxation was much heavier, and infinitely more galling than it is now. Under the Muhammadans it was worse still. They think that the Land Survey system was better. I shall shew that under the Cholas it was so intricate that the peasantry must in consequence have been absolutely at the mercy of the village chiefs. Again, whereas at the present day a native of India is as free to move about the country and exercise himself in trade with the whole world as an Englishman is in England, in former days he was confined to his own village and a very limited surrounding area by the absence of roads and communications, and by the terror of thugs and dacoits who robbed and murdered the traveller with impunity. A few other points will also be noticed.

I have said that the Hindu, by the habit of his race, seldom looks backwards into the past. We in England do. We travel by train, breakfasting, say, in London and lunching in Derby, the carriage comfortably warmed and running smoothly along, and we dream of the advance of the age, and the difference between the journey as it is accomplished now and what it would have been a hundred years ago. But how do we know anything about the then condition of things? Of course by our study of the facts of history as taught to us at school, and college, of contemporaneous records, of autobiographies, and historical novels. In a word we compare because we possess the means of comparison. Very few of these sources of information exist for the Hindu. Much might be obtained from a scientific study of ancient writings and from inscriptions, but these are not as a rule studied. And even here there must be comprehensive limitation. For if we may judge by their inscriptions the faculty of faithful history-writing has from the earliest ages been conspicuous by its absence in India. The Hindus of all ages appear to have cared little for the events of days beyond the limit of their own personal knowledge. The Muhammadans indeed have left us valuable records of their times, such as the history of Ferishta and many others; the Hindus, so far as I am aware, never. They think such records useless. When a thing is done it is done, and there is no need to write a book about it. Certainly the Hindus whom I have met have, as a rule, taken little or no interest in historical subjects. I was at one time in correspondence with the best educated Hindu officers of the Government as well as private gentlemen resident in all parts of the Madras Presidency on the subject of the antiquities and history of Southern India, a research which led to the publication of my two volumes on Madras Antiquities; and during the whole of the twenty-one years of my residence there I interested myself everywhere in old monuments and inscriptions. I found amongst the Hindus an almost universal want of interest in these subjects. They would take no trouble to decipher the inscriptions, and if a monument was of considerable antiquity it sufficed them to say that it had been erected by the gods. That was enough. Any myth would do, any fable or fairy story. To really arrive at the true circumstances seemed to them waste of time—foolishness.

It has often fallen to my lot, when camping out on duty, to have my tents pitched under a lofty hill, upon the topmost crags of which stood boldly out the bastions and towers of one of those grand old fortresses that dominate the surrounding country in so many parts of Southern India, and I have asked the townsfolk around me what they know about it. Very seldom I have heard some short tale regarding it, as that a prince or chief once threw his wife from one of the parapets; but more generally the answer has come "It is a fort." "Yes," I would reply, "I can see that for himself, but have you not *one* story about it? *No* legend of any fighting or siege? Have you no notion of who built it? or why? or when?" Almost always came the disheartening reply, "None." Sometimes I would get an answer similar to that given me at Karunguli in the Chingleput District. There is a large square rough-stone fort there, situated in the open plain. It was originally built by the Muhammadans about two centuries ago. It passed into the hands of the French in 1750, and in 1759 was taken by the British under Sir Eyre Coote. Orme's History contains an account of the siege, with a plan annexed to it. The attack lasted six days and the garrison capitulated and marched out with all the honours of war, colours flying and drums beating. I went one day into the village a few hundred yards away to see if I could find any trace left of the English batteries, opposite the clearly defined breach on the north wall. I found the place for which I had been searching, and then began to ask the village officers and the inhabitants of the houses round about whether there was any tradition in the village regarding this event. None whatever. No one knew or cared. "It was a fort"—that was all. But who built it? Answer, "It is said that it was built by Arjuna in the times of the Kurus and Pândiyas." Their ideas jumped back to the wars of the *Mahâbhârata*.

It is true that this ignorance of the real condition of their country in past days is not confined to the people of India. We in England are often singularly backward also in this respect. But we possess as a nation what I may term the historic faculty. We have contemporary records, written in all ages by people who thought, at the time, that the events of the day ought not to be entirely lost sight of by future generations. Some nations of ancient days possessed it—but not all. The Jews possessed it. The Egyptians apparently not. But I am not only referring to a record of political events, of dates and battles. I refer more to the general notion prevailing as to the former condition of the country. Story books and novels dealing with past days constitute the principal sources of information to a British schoolboy or young man. The Hindu has none such.

It is this want of the historic faculty which leads the Hindu into the land of dreams, the land of poetry, and here he is at home. He does dream of a Past, but the dream is in most cases a mere vision of non-realities. He dreams, as I said, of there having once been a time when all India from the Hindu Kûsh to Ceylon lay under the Imperial sway of magnificent monarchs of supreme power and dignity, the like of whom the world has never seen, under whose benignant and enlightened government flourished all the Arts and all the sciences in unparalleled splendour. He dreams that under this government the people were more free and less heavily taxed, that the taxes were somehow less burdensome, less irritating; that there was little or no oppression of the people by corrupt officials. As to the sciences, I once heard one of these dreamers, a young Brahman who spoke excellent English, declare in a lecture that the knowledge of medicine arose in ancient India as well as the knowledge of every other science; and that such was the power of diagnosis possessed by the ancient Hindu doctors that, whereas one of our poor ignorant latter-day surgeons is compelled to examine the person of a patient to ascertain the cause of his illness, in old India the leech could at once come to a right conclusion merely by touching the end of a stick pushed through a hole in a curtain by a person hidden behind it. There was similar excellence, he averred, in all branches of study.

That I am not exaggerating in my view of the notions which gain ground in the mind of the Hindus may be shewn by a very recent instance which any of my readers may verify for himself. It is a declaration of his belief by a highly educated and gifted gentleman—a "territorial Mahârâjah"—writing in the pages of the *Asiatic Quarterly Review* in January of last year, with reference to a paper on the "*Sovereign Princes of India and their relation to the Empire,*" by Sir R. Lethbridge.* The writer professes to be engaged on a retrospect based on the authority of the past history of the country, but for his history he goes to the ancient epic poems and even then totally misreads them. He says:

"In the halcyon days of Hindu sovereignty, this land of Bharata enjoyed the blessings of a peaceful reign, the Court of Ayodhya on the one hand, and the Court of Hastinapura on the other hand, having acted as centres of political supremacy, binding the vassal sovereigns by the common tie of patriotism towards their mother land, and loyalty towards their sovereign, recognized as such, by divine right. From the glimpses of political history we can gather on the authority of our ancient epics—the Râmâyana and the Mahâbhârata—we learn that every political act of great moment was, before its execution, proposed by the sovereign head and carried by the unanimous voice of the vassals. . . . . The war of the Mahabharata was another momentous act of politics that was brought about by the united voice of the subject sovereigns and vassals who were scattered about the length and breadth of this vast and glorious empire consisting of 56 Aryan Principalities (note, please, "*Aryan*"). Still later, when we come to Somnâth, we find the Hindu sovereigns assembled under a common banner, in the cause of their religion and country to oppose Mohamed of Ghazni." From these instances he argues that in ancient India there must have been one grand Imperial Constitution over all the land, with the chiefs forming the responsible Council of the sovereign, and he pleads for a re-establishment of this system. A little later he describes the political condition of the whole country as consisting of "the Imperial Majesty of India

* *Asiatic Quarterly Review*, Oct. 1895, p. 312.

and her vassal sovereigns united in holy relation." All this is a very pretty fancy, no doubt, but it appears to me to be simply untrue. Apart from the facts of the case, which are well known to the real student of Indian History, think for a moment how impossible in practice such a conception is. How would it be possible for a sovereign in South India to travel, merely in order to attend a Council at Ayodhyâ, all the length of India and back to his own territory at a time when there were no roads, and when he would have had to take with him an army for his protection? A couple of years' absence would have been necessary, and I have never yet read of any admission by Chola or Pândiyâ sovereigns that they were vassals of Ayodhyâ. The writer himself, no doubt conscious of the weakness of his position, is wise enough to speak of this system of vassalage as appertaining to "prehistoric" times, but he does not hesitate to use this supposititious prehistoric constitution as a plea for the introduction of a similar state of things in the reign of Queen Victoria.

Is it not time, then, for the English to teach the Hindus the real truth? Is it not almost a scandal—is it not productive of endless mischief—that, supposing these things to be untrue, we make no attempt to teach the people what the truth is?*

It is too late to influence by sound education the convictions of those already of mature age. The mischief has so far been done. But we can at least teach the facts of history to the younger generation; and thus secure that a just historical comparison, based on truth and not on a misunderstanding, may become possible for that great body of thinking men who, a few years hence, will be the guides of Hindu convictions throughout the length and breadth of the country.

* To make sure of my facts I have perused the Calendars of the University of Madras for last year. Before leaving India, animated by the same spirit that now possesses me, I pressed that University to further the study of the true history of the country. This was in answer to their request that I would name a special historical subject for the Master of Arts Degree examination. The University did not accept my views, but fixed for that special study *"The Italian Republics of the Middle Ages,"* and the paper set contained such questions as "What do you know of the sedition of the Ciompi and the Plot Marino Faliero?"

The Matriculation Examination contained an historical paper in which four questions related to Indian History, one only having reference to anything pre-European. The "First Arts" Examination contained no paper on history at all. The B. A. examination contained a paper on Greek and Roman History, one on Ancient and Mediæval Institutions, but all concerned with England, one on the History of the Middle Ages in Europe, and one on the History of Great Britain, poor India being totally neglected. And so with the M. A. examination, which deals with a multitude of abstruse subjects, and has papers on Carthaginian History, the Normans, Germany, but in which the Indian section contains only the history of English India in the last 100 years. I am glad to see however that they have encouraged the study of Indian numismatics, which leads to a study of history.

Ancient Indian Empire—a Myth.

My first attempt will be to combat the too often received idea that at some past date India consisted of one nation under one ruler. This appears to be contrary to the facts of history. India seems to have always been, as Europe has always been, a congeries of separate peoples, mostly living a life full of tribal and racial animosities and jealousies and constantly at war with one another. It is the nineteenth century alone that has seen the whole of this great country consolidated and unified under the peaceful rule of one sovereign; for even in the time of the Mogul sovereigns, who certainly were supreme, the country was in an exceedingly disturbed condition. At no time was there universal peace.

The very name "India" is a growth of little more than a century. Formerly Europeans spoke of Hindustân, but "Hindustân" did not mean India any more than "Hanover" means the present German Empire. The races were just as distinct, the languages just as various as the races and languages of Europe.

Let us look forward for a moment at the world as it may possibly be a couple of centuries hence. The whole of Europe has been unified under the rule of a single Emperor, the unification having been finally completed only about fifty years back. Is it possible to imagine the educated classes of that country, living in such widely separated tracts as the Highlands of Scotland and the mountains of the Morea, seriously believing that at some fairly recent period—the actual interval being to them a matter of no moment—all Europe had constituted a single realm, peaceful and happy under the sway of a single magnificent ruler? It will be said that such ignorance would be impossible. But it would be an exact parallel to the beliefs of the leaders of Hindu thought at the present day as to the past history of their country. Or take the case of Africa. Conceive that in another hundred years the whole of that great continent has come under the empire of one of the great European nations, and that tranquillity and freedom reigns from end to end of it. A very slight knowledge of history would enable the inhabitants to realize the condition of Africa in the nineteenth century—the constant warfare of races, the ghastly horrors of the slave-trade, the wanton destruction of human life, the massacres and slaughters of unoffending people by savage chiefs—chaos almost inconceivable, where in very truth might was the only right, and law was practically non-existent. And can it be conceived that the Government of the day would be so short-sighted as to allow the negroes, through pure ignorance of their past, caused by want of education, to believe that Africa, a century or two previous, had been the peaceful and happy possession of a universal monarch, under whom the single African nation had lived a life of Elysium? Yet this would only be a parallel to what our Government has done and is doing in India.

The Epic Poems.

The earliest inhabitants of India of whom we know anything were the so called Turanian tribes. These were pitilessly crushed and harassed by their Aryan conquerors, and called *Dasyus*, evil spirits, demons, barbarians, and as a self-governing race nothing remains to tell of their existence save the remnants of a few despised and outlawed tribes in the hill tracts. The invading Aryans looked on them as savages and cannibals, made slaves of them, and slaughtered them mercilessly. It is true that in the South of India the masses of the people are still probably pure Turanians, but after its conquest they never governed themselves, so far as we know, the royal races of that tract being of pure Aryan descent. (Note how the territorial Mahârâjah spoke of 56 *Aryan* principalities.)

The exact age of the great Epic Poems, the *Râmâyana* and *Mahâbhârata*, is not yet definitely decided. If they teach us anything at all historical, they prove nothing but the existence of constant wars of dynasties and races throughout the length and breadth of the continent. That Râma may have been a bold and successful conqueror is perfectly true, but how great was the area conquered and how long his dominion lasted is altogether conjectural. If he, a pure blood Aryan, actually conquered the Dakhan and the South, then the poems conclusively prove the existence at that period of hostile races, and their subjugation by an alien monarch of the North.

Do we find in the poems any claim of universal empire? Far from it. According to the *Râmâyana* (Book IV., Ch. 41), there were fourteen separate races inhabiting the country south of the Tungabhadra alone, *i.e.* the extreme south of the peninsula. And that these were not mere local tribes under one lord is proved by the fact that the writer includes not only Cholas, Pândiyas and Keralas, but also (I think erroneously) Kâlingas and Andhras. And to the north of this tract many works place the great Dandakâranya or waste country of Dandaka, a large area consisting of rocks, forests, and uncultivated plains, situated near the Godâvari river.

In the *Mahâbhârata* we find two branches of the local reigning family fighting savagely for the territory of Hastinâpura. They call in the aid of neighbouring chiefs, of whom there were many. Six different kingdoms are mentioned as existing in one tract on the Ganges, *viz.*, Hastinâpura, Mattra, Panchâla, Benares, Magadha, and Bengal. Krishna, the ally of the Pândavas, had a principality in Gujarât. Among the other allies are chiefs from the Indus, and from Kalingâ, south of Bengal. We hear also of the Bhîl Râja, south of the Jumna.

When the Pândavas left Hastinâpura, a very short distance sufficed to bring them to countries subject to aboriginal chiefs called Râkshasas or Asuras (demons). Ayodhyâ was only as far south-east as Allâhâbâd. Arjuna's exile leads us to more independent kingdoms, the Nâgas and Manipura. The Pândavas entered the service of the Virâta Râja, about 100 miles south of Delhi. It is evidently mere poetic license that makes the poem end with the conquest by Yudhishthira and his brethren of every Râja throughout the length and breadth of India.

The *Râmâyana* is a distinctly later poem, but there also we find that the whole country lay under the dominion of numbers of chiefs totally independent of one another. There is no pretence at any claim to universal sovereignty throughout the epic. The story concerns a small state with a limited area, and the neighbours are mentioned by name, Mithila (Tirhût), Girivraja (Râjgîr in Behar) the old capital of Magadha, the Bhîl Râja whose frontier was only 20 miles from Allahâbâd. Prayâga (Allahâbâd itself) was outside Râma's territory, so was Bandelkhand. The whole country south of the Jumna and Ganges was in the possession of aboriginal chiefs.

To come to more historical times we have the accounts of the Greek invasion of Northern India. Darius Hystaspes crossed the Indus in B.C. 521, and conquered and annexed to the Persian Empire the whole of the Panjâb and the Indus Valley. To the Persians succeeded the Greek Kingdom of Alexander and his successors. After the Greeks came the Scythian hordes and their kings, Huvishka and Kanishka.

When Alexander seized the country he found no lord paramount in Upper India. The Panjâb was under separate kings more or less at war with one another. Chandragupta and Puru of Magadha were local sovereigns ruling over a few vassal states in their immediate neighbourhood. Megasthenes (about B.C. 300) states that there were 118 nations in India, and mentions none of these as subordinate to Chandragupta. There was therefore no pretence at universal sovereignty at that time, and indeed a large portion of Upper India lay under foreign domination for 600 years, Greeks succeeding to Persians, and Tartars to Greeks.

After this we come to Asoka (B.C. 250 roughly); and as it is on his behalf that we hear the claims of universal empire put forward more often than on that of any other monarch, it is worth while to examine the matter a little closely.

Asoka.

We shall find that Asoka was by no means a universal *Chakravarti*. Quite the contrary. It is impossible that his monarchy could have extended beyond at most the limits of Hindustân proper. Chandragupta founded his monarchy by conquest after Alexander's invasion, and became overlord to many of the less important chiefs of that tract. Bimbasara succeeded him, and was followed by Asoka. In the later years of his life the latter became converted to Buddhism, and spread his doctrine far and wide over India, but it must not be supposed that he possessed also the temporal power over all that tract. To prove that this was not the case we have only to examine his own edicts where he mentions the names of contemporary neighbouring sovereigns.

In the thirteenth edict* he mentions his conquest of Kalingâ in the 9th year of his reign, and his resolve to make no further conquests. Kalingâ lay to the immediate south of Bengal. That it was a hard nut to crack is proved by Asoka's own declaration, that during the war 150,000 souls were carried off as prisoners or slaves, 100,000 were slain, and many times that number died. He deeply repented of all this terrific slaughter and suffering, and never again attempted a war of conquest.

In the second edict he mentions expressly "nations and princes that are his neighbours," such as the Cholas, the Pândiyas, the Satiyaputra, the Keralaputra, and the Yona (or Greek) king Antiochus, with his vassals. The Cholas and Pândiyas reigned in the Peninsula south of Madras, the Keralaputra in Malabar. The locality of the Satiyaputra is not clearly known, but lay probably to the north of the large southern kingdoms, possibly in the Dakhan. In the 5th edict Asoka mentions, besides his own subjects, the "Yonas, Kamboyas, Gandhâras, Rastikas, Pitinikas, and others which are my neighbours."

In the thirteenth edict, Asoka himself most distinctly states that his claim to any supremacy in India was a purely religious one. He says that the chiefest of conquests is "conquest through the Sacred Law. And that conquest has been made by the Beloved of the Gods both here in his empire and over all his neighbours, even as far as six hundred *yojanas,* where the king of the Yonas called Amtiyoka *dwells,* and beyond this Amtiyoka *where* the four kings *dwell.*" The names of these are given —Ptolemy, Antigonos, Magas and Alexander—they were at that time kings of Egypt, Macedonia, Cyrene, and Epirus. Mention of them clearly shows that Asoka claims no temporal sovereignty

* The quotations are throughout given from Hofrath von Bühler's *Asoka Edicts* in the *Epigraphia Indica*, vol. ii.

over their territories. And the king then goes on to mention, in the same sentence, the Cholas and Pândiyas. By analogy he claimed no sovereignty therefore at that date over Southern India. Then he mentions a number of separate nations, over whom similarly he claims no sovereign rights—the "Visas, Vajris, Yonas, Kamboyas, Nâbhitis, Bhojas, Pitinikas, Andhras, and Pulindas." Dr. Bühler considers that the Visas were the Bais Râjputs, and the Vajris the Vrijis of Eastern India. The mention of the Andhras, who held at least the Southern Kalingâ country, seems to prove that Asoka's temporal kingdom did not extend further south than Northern Kalingâ, *i.e.*, that it was confined to the limits of Bengal and the portion of the Kalingâ country which he had conquered—his only conquest. Lastly the king notes that he spread his doctrines by means of messengers. According to the Singhalese chronicle, the *Mahâvanso*, Mogaliputto, in the time of Asoka, sent missionaries to several tribes, and amongst these are mentioned some names not noted in Asoka's edicts, *viz.*, the Mahârattas and Aparântakas. This explains the existence of a rock edict of Asoka even so far south as North Mysore. The king claims no sovereign rights of any kind over that tract, but, earnest in spreading his kindly and benevolent doctrine over all India, he obtained permission of neighbouring kings to inscribe his edicts on rocks in their territory.

It is thus shown that Asoka held no universal empire, and that India, in his time as before, consisted of a large number of distinct nationalities, tribes and kingdoms.

India after Asoka.

This state of things was certainly not changed by the invasion of the Tartar Yueh Chi, and of the Scythian tribes, Huns or Sakas, who overran Upper India, and under Kadphises, Kanishka and Huvishka, established a dominion in that tract that lasted for some centuries with varying fortunes; being at its greatest about A.D. 50.

Contemporaneously with those Scythian inroads the sovereignty of Asoka's successors of the Maurya, Sanga, and Kanva dynasties came to an end, and we find the Andhras coming to the front on the Eastern coast. Did they then acquire or ever claim universal sovereignty? By no means. They seem to have been powerful, but their territories were not extensive, and they mentioned neighbouring kings in their inscriptions.

And so with the other dynasties of that period, Guptas and others. It is true that our information as to the condition of India until at least five centuries after our era is somewhat vague. But at Asoka's date, and after the downfall of the Andhras and our emergence into greater historical light, we find the Cholas and Pândiyas in possession of their territories, and never the slightest trace of any chief who claimed to be paramount over the rest. Indeed the very doubt and confusion probably arose from a disturbed condition of things, strife of races and the clash of contending arms, wars amongst neighbours, and inroads of savage tribes from over the mountains of the north.

The Hindu poems, grand and beautiful as some of them doubtless are, must not always be relied on for historical accuracy. Claims to universal monarchy on behalf of their chiefs are often made in poems and inscriptions, but on very insufficient grounds. I know of a fine spirited chronicle, the story of some chiefs in the Dakhan, where descriptions are given of the movements of their armies, their victories and conquests. They are said to have conquered Mâlava, Konkana, Drâvida, Kalingâ, Sindh, Bengal, Kosala, all the countries of India mentioned in the great epics. Their armies were as the sand of the sea in number, their cities were built of precious stones, their streets were paved with gold, the inhabitants invariably dressed in satins and silks. The king was a *Mahârâjâdhirâja Chakravarti*, or universal emperor of all India. When he moved to battle the sun was darkened with flights of his arrows, the tread of his elephants shook the earth to its foundations, so that even Indra trembled on his throne in Heaven. And so on. And all this was written about a small princeling who owned a little territory on the Krishnâ river about 50 miles square and never left it.

Vikramaditya.

Not long ago I heard a lecture delivered by a highly distinguished Indian official, in the course of which the speaker alluded to the prevalent belief in India as to the existence of at least two great emperors of India who possessed universal dominion. These were Asoka and Vikramâditya, the latter of whom is supposed to have introduced the Vikrama era, which has its epoch in B.C. 56. I have already disposed of Asoka, and will now for a few minutes discuss the myth of Vikramâditya. We know of very few kings of that name. There was a Vikramâditya, also called Harsha, of Ujjain, whose date apparently was not earlier than the fifth century A.D. One, and possibly two, of the Gupta kings of the fifth century adopted the name as a *biruda*, or second name; and then we come to certain kings of that name belonging to an equally local dynasty, the Western Châlukyas, in the country about Bombay and the Western Dakhan, between the years A.D. 1700 and 1126.

It is useless for present purposes to enquire too closely as to which of these princes was the original of the character around which all the romantic web of stories and legends and fancies has been weaved. Hiouen Thsang (about A.D. 630) mentions a prince of that name of unbounded liberality. Vikramâditya I. of the Western Châlukyas was a considerable monarch in his way,—a successful warrior, and a patron of learning. But nothing could be further from the truth than to suppose that either of these kings pretended to universal empire in India; and it appears fairly clear now that the 'Vikrama era' was not definitely founded by a king called Vikramâditya.

The real origin of the Vikrama era is lost in the mist of ages. Dr. Kielhorn has, in the pages of the *Indian Antiquary*, summarized in most scholarly manner a large number of Vikrama dates given in inscriptions, and for the assertions I am about to make I depend entirely on his careful and painstaking research. The earliest inscriptions in which the era is used, though *without giving it any name at all*, come from Eastern Râjputana, but for nearly 900 years after the epoch only 10 are known. The earliest of these occurs in A.D. 370, the last in A.D. 840. The period of the earliest is more than four centuries after the epoch. The first mention of the name *Vikrama* (not *Vikramâditya*, be it observed, but "*the time called Vikrama gone by*") is in the year A.D. 840-41, nine hundred years after the epoch, and 170 years after the time of Vikramâditya I. It is only in A.D. 992 that we first hear a "king Vikrama" in connection with the era, and this is in a poem. The use of the era seems to have been very sparing down to the year A.D. 1042, only 3 inscriptions being known which are expressly referred to the Vikrama era, and to have only gradually spread in later years. The tract where it is first found in use is, as before said, Eastern Râjputânâ. It spread to the north-east and east, to Kanauj, Gwalior, and Bandelkhand, and afterwards towards the south-west and south to Anhilvâd. It will be noted that this tract is altogether different from the territories ruled over by the Western Châlukyas, but that it includes the country of the Chaulukya and Vaghela princes of Anhilvâd.

Dr. Kielhorn lays particular stress on "the gradual change that may be observed in the phraseology of the dates in *Chaulukya* documents. The earliest of these (A.D. 985), 1000 years after the era, calls it simply *samvat*, "the year." In 1028 A.D. and 1090 we have *Vikrama samvat*, "the year." In 1028 A.D. and 1090 we have *Vikrama samvat*. In A.D. 1138 it is "The year of the illustrious Vikrama." Finally about A.D. 1200 we have, for the first time, "the year established by the illustrious Vikramâditya." This was amongst the same race over whom Vikramâditya I. had ruled more than 500 years earlier; ample time for a legend connecting him with the era to have grown up in consequence of the similarity of name, and the fact that the reign of that king had become associated with glorious traditions.

If any king named Vikramâdityâ had really established the era, we should expect of course to find his name associated therewith in the earliest dates extant, whereas it is never mentioned for, as far as we yet know, 1250 years.

After A.D. 1200 the usage is common, and we may fairly assume that by that time the inhabitants of that tract, Râjputânâ and Northern Bombay, had begun to believe in a legendary king named Vikramâditya who established the era to which they had been for so long accustomed. However it is possible that we may have to put the date of this general acceptance of the legend later still, for Dr. Kielhorn states that "over the largest part of the territories in which the era was used it was, down to Vikrama 1400 (A.D. 1342) styled the Vikrama era by poets only."

And now for the most probable theory yet advanced as to the origin of the name. Professor Kielhorn points out (*Ind. Ant.* XX. 470) that the years of the Vikrama era originally began in the autumn, with the month Kârttika (October-November). That is the season when in that tract the prolonged hot weather is over, the burning winds, the parched condition of the plains, the fierce dust storms of the summer are past. Welcome rain cools the air, vegetation bursts forth, and the whole of Nature arises "like a giant refreshed." It is the season when armies go forth to war. And the *Vikrama-kâla* is thus the poetic "war-time," "action time," for *vikrama* means a "stepping" "striding," or otherwise "heroism," "prowess." Long years afterwards the people connected the name with the name of a king Vikrama whom they supposed to have lived at that time. Later still they associated the celebrated king Vikramâditya with this epoch, being ignorant of his real date, and so the usage arose and became stereotyped. I may be permitted even to ask whether it is not possible that *vikrama* may be merely a synonym of our word, "current," as applied to an era. I quote from Professor Monier-Williams' Sanskrit Dictionary, where *vikrama* is translated "stepping or going beyond, stepping or striding over, going, walking, proceeding . . ." with other meanings that need not be referred to. In this sense the "Vikrama year" would be merely the "current year," the "running era."

LATER YEARS.

I may now pass onwards in my historical sketch. We have come down to about 500 years after the Christian era, and find no trace of a universal monarch. About this period we do hear of a very powerful sovereign King Silâditya of Kanauj. He seems to have held the whole of the north. But be it understood *only* the north. His attempt at conquest south of the Nerbudda failed entirely.

It is only in the extreme south that we find, down to comparatively recent dates, the ancient Aryan sovereignties remaining undisturbed by foreign invasion. They were subject to perpetual warfare amongst themselves, but down to Muhammadan times they retained with varying fortunes the territories occupied by them from at least the date of Asoka. These were the Cholas, Pallavas, Pândiyas, Keralas, Cheras and a few others of lesser importance. They held the South of India below the Dakhan. Further North, in the Dakhan country and the South of Bengal, there was a succession of separate sovereignties, the Andhra dynasty succumbing to the Pallavas, and the countries to the west falling under the dominion of Châlukya conquerors from Anhilvâd and Râjputânâ. The Châlukya kings mention a large number of races and kingdoms in their early inscriptions—for instance, Nalas, Mauryus, Sendrakas, Mâtangas, Katachchuris, Gangas, Alupas, Lâtas, Mâlavas, Gûrjaras, all of whom, one after another, fell under their dominion. Then came a great inroad of Châlukyas to the East, over which a branch dynasty ruled for four centuries, and further invasions by them of the Pallava and Chola countries to the south. Besides these we have powerful lines of local sovereigns in the Kâdambas, Râshtrakutas, Silâhâras, and Rattas, each in turn conquering and holding large tracts for definite periods.

In the eleventh century A.D. the Cholas of the south, arose to great eminence. They acquired the territories of the Eastern Châlukyas by a royal marriage—they finally destroyed the Pallavas, and for a time at least conquered and held the territories of the Pândiyas. A little later the Hoysala Ballâlas rose to power in the Maisûr country and the dominions of the Western Châlukyas, and then the Ganapati kingdom of Orangal arose, while the Pândiyas regained their territories, and the Cholas lost power.

But for a moment let us turn to the north. If perpetual strife and warfare between neighbouring princes had been the rule in the south, it was no less so in the tract which we have learned to call Hindustân. Race fell before race, nation before nation, dynasty before dynasty in bewildering confusion till the whole of that country fell under the sway of the invading Muhammadans.

Delhi was captured in A.D. 1193, and the whole of Northern India fell under Muhammadan sway. Early in the fourteenth century the Muhammadans swept into the Dakhan. They seized the territories of the kings of Devagiri and Orangal, and established themselves firmly, founding a dynasty called the Bahmanis, which claimed independence of Delhi. This again split up into five separate sovereignties, and in A.D. 1565 these, uniting, crushed for ever the last great Hindu kingdom of the south, that of Vijayanagar, which by that time had itself destroyed all the older Hindu dynasties.

And so for the first time in history we come to a period when India may possibly be said to have fallen under one rule. But this was not so in reality, for the Muhammadan chiefs established a succession of separate sovereignties, each one warring against the other, the whole against their own over-lord. Their domination also was an alien, not a Hindu domination. There has never been in all history, amongst the Hindus, anything but a perpetual warfare of races, king against king and tribe against tribe.

And so the cherished theory of a universal empire falls to the ground; and it is to be hoped that it will, ere long, be consigned to the limbo of all other false and mistaken theories. The mistake has arisen partly in consequence of historical ignorance, and partly in consequence of the equal government of the English, under which all historic feuds and racial hatreds have been merged in the attempt to establish universal justice for all inhabitants of India alike, from north to south, and from sea to sea.

Taxation.

Let me now turn to the question of taxation under Hindu sovereigns. We hear loud outcries sometimes against the English taxation of India. Hindus of light and leading are bold to declare that under their old chiefs the people were less heavily taxed, and that in themselves the taxes were less burdensome and less irritating. Was this so?

I will turn to the most long-lived Hindu sovereignty with which I am acquainted, a sovereignty which certainly existed as far back as B.C 250, and which was only finally crushed by the Muhammadan invaders in comparatively very recent days—I allude to the Chola Dynasty of the south of India, which had its capital at Tanjore.

Through all this long period it was governed by a succession of Aryan Princes, claiming to belong to the "Solar Race," and we hear of no interruption to this dynastic autocracy. Unlike most other parts of India, therefore, it will yield us an excellent picture of purely Hindu government if we can arrive at the administrative details. Fortunately we are to a certain extent enabled to do so, for on the walls and plinth of the great temple at Tanjore has been sculptured a very lengthy series of royal grants and royal edicts of the best days of the Chola Kingdom, the 11th and 12th centuries A.D., and these have been lately given to the European world in the splendid volumes of the Archæological Survey published by Dr. E. Hultzsch. Dr. Hultzsch is one of the most painstaking and accurate epigraphists of the day, and the exactness of his translations may be depended upon. Let us see then what we can gather regarding the system of taxation under the Hindu kings. At p. 117 of Dr. Hultzsch's volume* we have a list of taxes, due by the inhabitants of a village and made over to certain persons by royal grant, in the eleventh century A.D. The list runs as follows:—all kinds of revenue (âya) including the tax in money, two taxes whose names are given in the Tamil but the meaning of which is not yet known, tax for the village watchman, tax for the village accountant, tax for unripe fruit in the month of Kârttigai, tax on looms, tax on oil-mills, tax on trade, another untranslatable tax, tax on goldsmiths, tax on animals, tax on tanks, tax on watercourses, tolls, another untranslatable tax, tax on weights, fines for selling rotten drugs, tax on shops, tax on salt, tax on elephant-stalls, tax on horse-stables. There are probably others also, but the inscription is partly broken away in one place.

Here is another list of the same period in the same locality, from which we can supplement the former, and it must be noted that all these are new and separate imposts, since I omit reference to taxes already mentioned:—*Nâdâtchi, nîrâtchi,* (whatever these may be), one *nâli* of rice for every platter, one *nâli* of rice on each day sacred to the worship of ancestors, tax on weddings, tax on washermen's stones, tax on potters, rent for use of water, collections of leaves, brokerage, tax on neatherds.

And here again is another list of the same period from a fresh source: Tax for the maintenance of Police; a rice-tax paid every year in the month of Kârttigai; a special tax levied per head on all belonging to the Jain religion; fees in the nature of stamp-duty on documents; a tax leviable for the support of the Prime Minister.

Now was this state of things exceptional? Certainly not, for lest it may be supposed that the Chola Kings were more grasping than other representatives of the other Hindu dynasties in the matter of the taxation of their subjects, I proceed to show what the taxation of the Indian citizen appears to have been at the time when the Greeks visited India (about B.C. 300) and also shortly before the English took over the country, so that we shall obtain an insight into his condition in all ages.

* Archæological Survey of India. *South Indian Inscriptions.* Vol. II., p. 117.

We find from the description of Palibothra, modern Patna, given by the Greek traveller Megasthenes, that the citizens of that town must have been greatly harassed by the provisions enforced by their ruler for the purpose of filling his treasury. At that early date there was a regular Government registration of all births and deaths for purposes of taxation. The buyers and sellers of goods in the bazaars were not left to themselves as they are now, but a State officer was appointed to watch all transactions, however petty, and seize for the State one-tenth of the price of everything sold. Fraud in the payment of this tax was punished by death. Other officers, in the nature of police, exercised general supervision. The State could not even leave the manufacturers alone, for since for its own purposes it had to encourage sales, so equally it was led to unnaturally force the supply. This meant that artizans must never be idle; and so, Megasthenes tells us, there were officers of State appointed to superintend all arts and industries to prevent negligence on the part of the workers.* Can anything be imagined more prying, inquisitorial, or irritating, than this system of an army of paid spies bent on forcing every branch of trade and seizing part of the proceeds of every petty sale? Think of the overwhelming opportunity for bribery and corruption which the system afforded. For every three or four shops must have been appointed a petty official with almost unlimited power, whose protection and countenance could be easily bought, and whose capacity for annoying was infinite. Being probably paid by results of sales he lay under a direct inducement to oppress and victimize the shopkeeper and artizan. The result may be easily conceived.

Here then we have taxation by Hindu rulers at widely different epochs, separated by an interval of twelve centuries. We will glance at the system of taxation by another Hindu ruler, Chikka Deva Râya of Mysore, two centuries ago. He maintained not only all the old taxes at that time existent but actually invented twenty new ones, some of which have at least the merit of being ingenious. Three are specially deserving of notice.

(1) Two per cent. was permanently added to the assessment all over the country to re-imburse the treasury for loss by defective coins. (2) When a man rented a village and engaged for payment of a fixed sum to the State, if his actual receipts fell short of this total he levied a contribution on his farmers. But the king fixed as a permanent tax the largest contribution ever so levied, in addition to the assessment. (3) If a farmer sold his grain in the village or neighbourhood he escaped payment of tolls. Therefore

* Strabo XV., 1, 50. (M'Crindle's *Ancient India*, p. 87.)

the king imposed a cash payment per plough all over the country to compensate for this supposititious loss.

All this grinding tyranny lasted down to the times of the English. In the Coimbatore District in 1799,* Major MacLeod found the following imposts in full force and effect,—*over and above the Land tax :*

1. Tax on potters.
2. „ payable by persons wearing caste-marks on their fore-head.
3. Fees levied on stalls at weekly fairs.
4. Tax on dyed stuffs.
5. „ on ghee.
6. „ on tobacco.
7. „ on grain heaps.
8. „ on chunam.
9. „ on watchmen (*taliyâris*).
10. „ on agricultural-irrigation watchmen (*nirgantis*).
11. „ on keepers of pack-bullocks.
12. „ on dancing-girls.
13. „ on overseers of labour (*maix-tries*).
14. „ on immoral persons.
15. Rents for lotus leaves.
16. Rents for gardens in back-yards of houses, and in plantations on river banks.
17. Fines on cattle grazing in fields.
18. Rents for young palmyra nuts.
19. Rents for tamarinds.
20. Rents for use of soapstone or pot-stone.
21. Rents for betel-nuts.
22. Fees for the measurement of grain, necessitated by the sharing system.
23. Taxes on offerings at a sacred temple.
24. Levies made for the poor, or poor-rate.
25. Taxes on agricultural hoes.
26. State exaction of a portion of the fees paid by villagers to their village officials (this in itself another well recognized tax).
27. Tax on sale of cattle.
28. „ on cattle-stalls.
29. „ on water-lifts.
30. „ on fisheries.
31. „ on looms.

(All these five as well as many others are old Chola taxes and evidently survived during the intervening centuries.)

32. A tax such as the third of those alluded to above as having been introduced by Chikka Deva Râya of Mysore.
33. Levies made on ryots for expenses of the Divisional Officer (Tahsildar). (These were probably very onerous.)
34. An additional payment enforced on every ryot at his first payment of instalment of Land Revenue.
35. A plough-tax.
36. Tax on houses.
37. „ on shops.
38. „ on carpenters.
39. „ on blacksmiths.
40. „ on goldsmiths.
41. „ on papermakers.
42. „ on dyers.
43. „ on shoemakers.
44. „ on barbers.
45. „ on washermen.
46. „ on oil-mills.
47. „ on pack-bullocks.
48. „ on salt pans.
49. „ on salt manufacturers.
50. „ on iron-smelters.
51. „ on indigo-makers.
52. „ on drawers and distillers of fermented palm juice.
53. „ on boatmen.
54. „ on carts.

* See the *Coimbatore District Manual*, p. 172, etc.

55. Tax on manufacturers of beaten rice.
56. „ on basket makers.
57. „ on pedlars.
58. „ on cattle and sheep (per head).
59. Tax on blanket and carpet weavers.
60. „ on mat makers.
61. „ on stone masons.*

Enquiry showed, as might of course have been assumed, that all kinds of fraud and corruption were rife. Village officers would give nominal leases of land to servants of the farmers, so as to enable them to escape the house-tax; for farmers were free of house tax, while their own servants were taxed on the huts they lived in. This house-tax varied in every village, sixteen different rates being found for blacksmiths and goldsmiths, and eighteen in the case of carpenters. It was found that taxation rested chiefly on the poorest who could not sufficiently bribe the tax-gatherer and village official, the richer people in great measure escaping. The tax on shops was made so comprehensive that a man was made to pay for a market-basket, a leather grain-bag, and even for the pack he fastened on to his bullock when going to the fair. Women who squatted by the roadside selling betel, tobacco, and petty wares in baskets were taxed at rates varying from Rs. 3-8-5 (a star pagoda) to nine and a half annas.

Besides all these there were the harassing transit-duties on all goods at innumerable chaukis, or toll-houses, established throughout the country. In 1801 the Madras Board of Revenue reported that this system of transit duties was most pernicious, and that the native tax-gatherers wrung from the people at least twice as much as they paid into the Treasury. They called it "a great engine of oppression." Almost all these taxes have been swept away by the English Government, even the payment of ordinary tolls being no longer demanded.

In the year 1853 the Madras Native Association presented a petition to the Committee of the House of Commons appointed to inquire into Indian affairs, in which they implored that the people might be relieved from at least one branch of this gigantic taxation, which was then called "moturfa," a name we received from the

* I am anxious not to exaggerate. Some few of these taxes remain, though in other forms, but according to the fairest analysis that I can make with my present lights, 45 taxes have clean gone. One, fines for cattle grazing on fields, comes under the head of criminal revenue as fine for proved trespass. I include four under modern income-tax in so far as concerns the richer classes, the poorer paying nothing, though all were formerly taxed. Houses and shops pay no tax to the State, but they are taxed for purely local expenditure in municipal towns and village unions, for streets, lighting, sanitation, and the like. And so carts and bullocks which use the roads. In the case of seven others (Nos. 3, 18, 19, 20, 21, 30, 48) the State in some shape or other derives some income at the present day, though one (No. 3) is solely devoted to local expenditure. I include the tax on salt-pans amongst these, though under the present system there is no salt-tax, the revenue being derived from a Government monopoly of the trade.

Muhammadans. The Petitioners' own words described this moturfa as "a tax on trades and occupations embracing weavers, carpenters, all workers in metals, all salesmen, whether possessing shops, which are also taxed separately, or vending by the roadside, etc., some paying imposts on their tools, others for permission to sell, extending to the most trifling articles of trade, and the cheapest tool the mechanic can employ; the cost of which is frequently exceeded six times over by the moturfa under which the use of them is permitted."*

Mr. Dykes, Collector of Salem, reported to the Select Committee not only that the taxes were oppressive in themselves, but that they even varied in each district and in every village, and that their assessment was in the highest degree abitrary, so that there was no security anywhere. The villager could only submit or bribe the officials, and this of course he did freely. Whenever an energetic trader increased his business the tax-gatherer came down on him for increased payments. "If," Mr. Dykes said, "the trader was a man of any sense he bought off the village authorities and did not get his assessment raised, the extent of his dealings not being reported." The Commissioners pointed out that this system of taxation, as regarded the weavers, was "more than usually inquisitorial, as the amount varies with the number of looms employed by each payer; houses were frequently entered in order to discover concealed looms, as the Indian loom is easily dismantled and put away." The tax was most grossly irregular also. For instance, in the Tanjore district, thickly populated, overrun with the Brahman and priestly element, where the village folk are exceptionally intelligent—the village officers also—the tax paid to Government by 232,321 payees amounted to three annas per head; while at the same time in Kurnool, a country of sparse population with inhabitants generally dull and unintelligent, the rate per head, for 12,104 payees, was Rs. 4-10-0. How much per head one wonders, did the clever Tanjore village-officers receive for themselves for the favour of concealing the dealings of the traders?

Here is a still further list of taxes (altogether independent of those mentioned above and of the land-tax) which I found in the Government office of my last District, Bellary. It embraces merely a few items of village taxation collectable at so recent a date as 1835.

1. Taxes exacted on the occasion of marriage:

(*a*) From bride.

(*b*) From bridegroom.

* Quoted, as are many other passages, from the admirable volume of Mr. Srînivâsa Râghavaiyangâr, Inspector General of Registration at Madras, entitled "Memorandum of the Progress of the Madras Presidency during the past Forty Years."

2. Tax called *Handertaneky* for erecting marriage pandals or pavilions.
3. „ called *Woodeky* on widows' re-marriage.
4. „ called *Bediki* on marriage of women to men while their own husbands are still alive.
5. „ collected from persons breaking the rules of their caste.
6. „ on re-admission to caste after having been expelled.
7. „ leviable on appointment of a person to be a priest of the Jangam caste.
8. „ called *Puttam kaniki*, or tax leviable on a person succeeding to the office of priest.
9. „ leviable from people of the Sâtâni caste, who perform worship in the lesser temples.
10. „ called *Guggalam*, or a tax on pilgrims who return successfully from pilgrimages and perform the vows they have made.
11. „ on ovens used by washermen.
12. „ on Government lands held on favourable tenure (*inâms*):

    (*a*) Tax at 2¼ seers of rice for every crop irrigated well by the use of one machine for raising the water (*kapila*).

    (*b*) Tax at a bundle of rice-straw in grain for every field irrigated under tanks.
13. „ on fermented liquors (toddy and arrack).

    (*a*) On the stills.

    (*b*) On the retail shops.

These taxes were regularly collected by the State, and the account from which I extracted the list was one of the ordinary treasury papers showing the amounts that had been paid into the Government office in the Bellary District during the year in question.

Let me now state what is our modern British system of taxation. It may be summarized in the words of the author of the Coimbatore District Manual. Speaking of the land revenue he writes, "Every modification has been entirely in favour of the ryot. . . . Roughly speaking the progress of the system has been from comparative restriction to almost absolute freedom . . . from a practice of sharing profits even on the ryot's capital to entire relinquishment of everything except the fixed assessment, from a somewhat inquisitorial system to complete non-interference with individuals." (*Op. cit.*, p. 92).

We have assessed the land-revenue at so much per acre of cultivated land, the measurement of which is fixed by actual survey. As regards the ratio of the Government assessment to the gross produce of the land Mr. Srinivâsa Râghavaiyangâr shows in his "Memorandum" that the rates are at present between one-fourth and one-fifth for irrigated lands, and between one-fourth and one-sixth for unirrigated lands—"in the case of lands in the poorer dry districts it is very much less." Besides this there is the village-service cess, taking the place of all the fees formerly exacted from the ryots by the village officials, and the local-fund land-cess for the upkeep of all the roads, hospitals, dispensaries, bridges and other district works. Both are charged on the assessment at so much per rupee of land revenue. These three cesses are, in the village accounts, lumped into one charge, and this one charge is what the ryot has to pay. It is fixed and definite, and this single payment is all with which he is ever troubled. He pays it moreover, by easy instalments, the periods of which are settled so as to fall at a time when, by sale of produce, the farmer is in the best position to meet the demand. The higher-class merchants now pay the income-tax, and the income-tax alone. There is no other direct State taxation, though there is local taxation to provide funds wholly spent on local requirements and improvements. For the few years between the abolition of the *moturfa* and the institution of the income-tax, the latter class paid absolutely no taxes whatever to the State. They subscribed nothing to the maintenance and government of the country. The income-tax moreover, is very moderate, all the poor being entirely free. It is only the rich who pay, and as compared with the system of taxation under Hindu governments, the tax, though certainly inquisitorial and unpopular, is beyond all question lighter and less onerous. The professional and trading classes are, as well expressed by the author of the "Memorandum," "bound to contribute their fair share to the public burdens, and therefore this solitary tax is quite sound in principle. The people are getting accustomed to the tax," and it is only sheer ignorance of what they suffered in the past that makes them accept it otherwise than gladly. Remembering that these classes pay no land-revenue we find that the people are thus subject individually to one solitary State tax under the present British administration. Let anyone compare this with the taxation under Hindu administration as given above, and then say whether the masses of the people are worse off now than they used to be.

Land-Revenue.

My next point, one which will not occupy much space, is the system of revenue land-survey and assessment under the native chiefs. Bitter complaints are sometimes raised against extortions practised by the native subordinate officials of our Revenue Survey and Settlement Department (not against the English remember). But it appears to be entirely forgotten that the old Hindu Kingdoms had similar institutions, only that they were so elaborate, intricate and minute, that no ordinary ryot could possibly understand them. There must have been a far larger army then of supervisors, clerks and measurers than under British administration. And if there is corruption amongst these gentry to-day we may well imagine what it was in those days, and how the poor farmer—quite at their mercy for details, and holding his land, not direct from the State, but merely as one of a number living in a village which paid a lump sum—must have been fleeced. The village officials paid their demand, and then came down on the farmers to make good the whole amount, whatever may have been the state of the season. At the present day the farmer in ryotwari tracts has a Government lease which gives him the details and total of all that he has to pay, including cesses; and education in at least the three R's is so much encouraged that he can read this lease, check the figures, and so secure himself against increased demand. Moreover they have English officers at hand to whom they can appeal for protection in case of any attempt at corrupt practices on the part of their village officers, and of this privilege they make free and constant use.

Here is the Revenue survey system of the Cholas as disclosed to us by an inscription on the Tanjore Temple (*p. 62, of Dr. Hultzsch's volume alluded to above*):

"The village of Iraiyânsêri contains, according to measurement, twelve measures of land, one half, two twentieths, one fortieth. and one three hundred and twentieth; $\frac{1}{320}$ of one quarter and three eightieths; and $(\frac{1}{320})^2$ of three quarters and one twentieth. There have to be deducted three quarters of a measure of land free from taxes, two twentieths, one eightieth and one hundred and sixtieth; $\frac{1}{320}$ of one half, and three twentieths; $(\frac{1}{320})^2$ of three twentieths, one hundred and sixtieth and one three hundred and twentieth; $(\frac{1}{320})^3$ of three eightieths; and $(\frac{1}{320})^4$ of three quarters and one twentieth; consisting of the village site, the site of the houses, the Pariah quarter, the watercourse called the Kannan channel, and the other channels which pass through this village and irrigate other villages, the village threshing-floor of this village, the ponds of this village and their banks, the sacred temple in this village and its sacred court, and the sacred bathing pond of the god. There remain eleven measures of land, three quarters and one hundred and sixtieth; $\frac{1}{320}$ of one half, two twentieths and three eightieths; $(\frac{1}{320})^2$ of one half, two twentieths and three eightieths; $(\frac{1}{320})^3$ of three quarters, four twentieths, one hundred and sixtieth and one three hundred and twentieth; and $(\frac{1}{320})^4$ of four twentieths.

The revenue paid as tax is one thousand one hundred and sixty-nine *kalam*, two *tûni*, two *nâri* and one *uri* of paddy (rice in the husk) which has to be measured by the *marakkâl* called *Adavallân*."

We thus see that the tax was imposed in lump on the whole village, and that the several farmers were absolutely at the mercy of the village elders as to their individual shares. When disputes arose it would seem very easy with such an elaborate system of measurement to confuse the minds of the village councillors, however anxious they may have been to decide aright, or to entirely befog the intellect of the aggrieved cultivator. Weights and measures varied in every village, and even if the amount of *marakkâls* of grain payable were at last definitely settled, the intriguing village official could take refuge in the difference between the *Adavallân marakkâl* and the local measure of the same name.

Now for all this, what have we substituted? We deal, as I have said, direct with each cultivator, the village accountant being merely the record-keeper. Each ryot has his paper shewing precisely how much he has individually to pay to the State in cash as land-revenue. And in place of this supremely confusing system of measurement we have one which would describe the village in question thus:—Total so many acres, assessment so many rupees; deduct waste and communal land so many acres, assessment so much; taxable remainder so many acres, so much assessment. Finally our acre is a fixed measure, and the village officers are furnished with necessary chains, so that no mistake is possible. Which system conduces most to the welfare and contentment of the Indian farmer?

Let it be remembered that here I am only referring to the condition of the agricultural classes, not of the Brahman, the large land-owner, or artizan.

The practice of a Government dealing with a village as a whole creates a vast amount of unhappiness in a place where the head-men are, as is unfortunately too often the case, unscrupulous or rapacious, for the individual lies entirely at their mercy. He has to pay whatever his chiefs choose to demand. But the whole village system lasted from the earliest days with which we are acquainted all through the days of Government by the Hindu kings, all through the Muhammadan period, down to the first quarter of this century.

The system of payment in kind also gives rise to an infinity of evils; but it has been the system uniformly enforced by the Hindu Governments. The late Dewân of Pudukottah, Mr. Seshiah Sâstri, C.S.I., has shewn up the evils of this practice in his Report on the administration of that State for 1879-80 (*Para.* 160). Though somewhat detailed I cannot refrain from recording some extracts, since my own experience coincides precisely with that of the writer. It discloses a system which must have been productive of infinite misery, suffering, injustice, and wrong. I have taken the liberty of translating his technical vernacular terms into English. The system was one where the crop was shared, in kind, between the farmer and the State; the term is "Amâni"; I translate this "share-system."

"(a) The Ryots *having no heritable or transferable property* [note this] never cared to cultivate the share-system lands in due season. . . . To prevent this a penal agreement is forced from them to the effect that they would not fail to cultivate the share-system lands first.

"(b) As soon as the ears of the grain make their appearance an army of watchers . . . is let loose. . . .

"(c) When the crop arrives towards maturity it is the turn of the Government village officers . . . to go round the fields, and note down estimates of the crop. That there is considerable wooing and feeing at this stage goes for the saying. *As in other matters, so in this, the race is to the rich and woe to the poor.*

"(d) As soon as the village-officers have done . . . down come special estimators from the Government divisional offices to check the first estimate. Their demands have equally to be satisfied. Then comes the business of obtaining permission to cut and stack the crops. . . .

"(e) Then comes the threshing and division of the grain on the threshing-floor. What takes place then may be imagined. If the outturn is less than the estimate, *the ryot is made responsible for the difference without more ado. If it is more, woe be to the estimators.* . . . During all this time the unpaid army of watchers continues on duty [being maintained and bribed, of course, by the unfortunate ryot, who in case of failure is liable to ruin by false accusations].

"(f) Now the Government grain is removed to the granaries. Is all danger over now? By no means. A fresh series of frauds commences. . . . The half-famished village watchman . . . mounts guard, and he and the village headmen are held personally responsible for any deficiency which may occur on the remeasurements of grain *out* of the granary. It often happens that the poor watchman . . . helps himself from time to time . . . [Then comes the day of reckoning, and] there is crimination and recrimination without end, the watchman charging the village heads, and the village heads the watchman. The Government officials . . . come down heavily on both, and often both are ruined. . . .

"(g) Time passes and the month denoting favourable markets comes round. There now remains the business of disposing of the Government grain from the granaries. Simple as it may appear, enormous difficulty is experienced, and we have to face another series of frauds, now on the part of the higher Government officials. Tenders are invited but only few come and bid low. Tenders are again invited, but to no better purpose. . . ."

And so the disheartening story goes on, a story of fraud and deceit and corruption, where the weaker, *i.e.*, the poor villager, always goes to the wall.

When Mr. Seshiah Sâstri took charge of the Pudukottah State in 1878 he states that "the cry was plunder and extortion everywhere."

This, then, furnishes us with a practical modern example of the state of the agricultural villages under the Hindu system. In saying this I disclaim absolutely all intention of unduly disparaging native methods. There was a good side, doubtless, as well as a bad. So there was in England during the period of the barons, with which historically the condition of India in days before the English may be compared. But no Englishman would like to go back to the old slavery: and it is my profound conviction that, if the Hindu really knew what India was like in old days, he, like the Englishman, would be more ready than he is at present to welcome modern methods.

But now another question. Was the amount of land revenue exacted by the State under the old Hindu and Muhammadan Governments greater or less than at the present day? The English take from ¼ to ⅙th. Mr. Srînivâsa Râghavaiyangâr points out that there is ample evidence to prove that the land-tax usually taken by both Hindu and Muhammadan sovereigns was fully one-half the gross produce. Whether it be true or not we have no means of knowing, but Strabo (xv. i, 40) declares that in the time of Megasthenes the Hindu sovereign, possibly he of Palibothra, claimed the ownership of the entire land, "and the husbandmen till it on condition of receiving one-fourth of the produce" (McCrindle, "*Ancient India*," p. 84). Dr. Burnell, in his "*South Indian Palæography*," writes:—"The inscriptions at Tanjore shew that the indigenous Chola kings of the 11th century took about half the produce." The native Hindu dynasties in the Northern Circars appear also to have taken half, and this rule remained in force in several estates and principalities which never, or only for a very short time, fell under actual Muhammadan domination—the Zamindâri of Râmnâd for instance. Under the Vijayanagar Hindu kings it was the same, and here we have the direct personal knowledge of the Jesuit Fathers to guide us. The Jesuit Madras

Mission Reports contain the following passages:—"The King or Grand Nâyakar of Madura has but a few domains which depend immediately on him, that is to say which form his property. . . . All the other lands are the domains of a multitude of petty princes, or tributary lords; these latter have each in his own domains the full administration of the police and of justice, if justice there is at all; *they levy contributions which comprise at least the half of the produce of the lands*. . . . The Grand Nâyakars . . . are themselves tributaries of Vijayanagar, to whom they pay, or ought to pay, each one an annual tribute of from 6 to 10 millions of francs. But they are not punctual in this payment; often they delay and sometimes refuse insolently; then Vijayanagar arrives, or sends one of his generals at the head of a hundred thousand men to enforce payment of all arrears, with interest, *and in such cases, which are frequent, it is the poor people who are to expiate the fault of their princes; the whole of the country is devastated, and the population is either pillaged or massacred.*" That was the Hindu method all over Southern India as late as the 17th century.

As to the Mahratta chiefs of Tanjore in 1683 we have a letter of another Jesuit missionary: "Ekoji appropriates four-fifths of the produce. This is not all, instead of accepting these four-fifths in kind, he insists that they should be paid in money; and as he takes care to fix the price himself much beyond that which the proprietor can realise, the result is that the sale of the entire produce does not suffice to pay the entire contribution. The cultivators then remain under the weight of a heavy debt: and often they are obliged to prove their inability to pay by submitting to the most barbarous tortures. It would be difficult for you to conceive such oppression, and yet I must add that this tyranny is more frightful and revolting in the Kingdom of Gingee. For the rest this is all I can say, for I cannot find words to express all that is horrible in it."

I continue to quote from the "*Memorandum.*" After showing that the land-revenue enacted in the south two centuries ago was almost inconceivable, the author writes:—"In other parts of the peninsula the revenue taken by other sovereigns was equally great, if not greater. In Orissa it appears that in the 12th century the Gangetic dynasty had a land-revenue of about £450,000, or a little less than three times the revenue derived by the British Government from the same province, while the purchasing power of the rupee was then 8 times of what it is now." And this is not all, for there is far more land now paying revenue than was the case in those days. Sir William Hunter's *Orissa* may be advantageously consulted on this point.

Now for the Muhammadan Emperors, and amongst others the best of them all, the wise and beneficent Akbar.

Akbar laid down a principle for regulating the land assessment thus:—

"There shall be left for every man who cultivates his lands as much as he requires for his own support till the next crop be reaped, and that of his family and for seed. This much shall be left to him, *what remains is the land-tax and shall go to the public treasury.*" The farmer is entitled to nothing but to be kept alive and be enabled to put down the next crops. Which means that he is to be kept alive really in order that, like a beast of burden, he may work for the State for the whole period of his existence. Is this an exaggeration?

The *Hedaia* states that it is not lawful to exact more than half the produce for the State treasury—" but the taking of a half is no more than strict justice and is not tyrannical, because, as it is lawful to take the whole of the person and property of infidels and distribute them among the Mussulmen, it follows that taking half their incomes is lawful *a fortiori.*"

Akbar abolished many vexatious taxes, and, to his honour be it said, fixed the land-tax at about one-third of the gross produce. But his successors re-imposed all the abolished taxes. And owing to their system of taking tribute from chiefs, leaving the latter to screw all they could out of the unfortunate farmer and merchant, there was never any comfort, nor justice for these. They were fleeced and fleeced and fleeced again, and when they could not pay, were subjected to barbarous tortures.

When I was treating of land mensuration just now, I alluded to the Chola calculations of the " marakkâl called Adavallân" shewing that there were other marakkâls in existence, and I contrasted that with the English measurement, the fixed and unalterable acre. Now Akbar and his successors measured by the *biga*, and whatever Akbar's views may have been as to the area of a *biga*, his successors, and especially the local chiefs, enhanced their revenues by introducing a *biga* of smaller and still smaller size; so that it is a fact that in the provinces of Agra and Delhi the *biga* was gradually reduced till it measured only one-third of its former dimensions. This trebled the revenue, and still the ryot was bullied and tortured if he did not pay.

The revenues of the Moghul Emperors have been carefully investigated by the late Mr. Edward Thomas, a very careful and reliable authority, and Mr. Srinivâsa Râghavaiyangâr says in a note (p. 13) that "the figures seem almost fabulous" . . . "the tax would represent a much larger proportion of the produce than one-half. . . . . In the beginning of the present century the tax (in Orissa) represented nearly 5-6ths of the gross produce, and the cultivators were left only the barest means of subsistence and often not even that." It was impossible to realise such a revenue, but those in power took all they could get.

The history of the few years of English administration has been a history of abolition of taxes, removal of all hindrances to the ryots' freedom, institution of means by which they can obtain justice and protection against oppressors, and steady reduction of the very heavy land-assessment. I will not weary my readers by entering into the various stages by which the present condition of things in India has been arrived at. My purpose is only to point out from historical facts what the condition of the agricultural population *was*. They themselves know what it *is*. And the learned classes, when they consider the condition of India at various periods, should not omit to notice the great mass of the population, viz., the agriculturists.

Condition of the People.

I have alluded to the perpetual fighting and wars that harassed the country and carried ruin and devastation into all corners of the nations, and I am anxious now to show what effect these constant disturbances had on the poor people of the towns and villages. For we need not consider the great Râjahs and their tributaries. A war may have been very glorious and splendid in its dynastic results, but what about the farmers and cultivators and artisans—the bulk of the population? It may be thought that wars were, as at present amongst civilized nations, confined to the king and his soldiery, but in India that was by no means always the case. It is true that Megasthenes, according to Diodorus (ii. 36), stated that in his time the tillers of the soil were not interfered with by contesting armies; but such humane forbearance was not the rule in all ages, as we shall presently see. War often meant the ruthless slaughter of unoffending peasants and citizens, the destruction of their towns and villages, and wholesale devastation of all cultivable area.

Wherever we look back there is fire and sword in the country. In the earliest days the destruction of the Dravidian tribes by the conquering Aryans. After the Aryan conquest, we have, if historical at all, the terrible wars of the *Mahâbhârata* and the virtual annihilation, by secret massacre as well as open war, of all the heroes of the epic. Then the *Râmâyana*, and Râma's conquest of the Dakhan and slaughter of the people. Coming to the domain of history proper, we read of the inroads of the Greeks, the Scythians, the Yueh-chi; in Asoka's reign the terrible slaughter in that monarch's bloodthirsty years, when he conquered part of Kalingâ and confessed that in doing so he had carried into slavery 150,000 souls, had slain 100,000, and had been the cause of the death of many times that number in addition. After this there is never a period without its wars of dynasties and nations ever harassing the peaceable inhabitants of the different tracts. Whenever a king was successful he boasts of having utterly destroyed the enemy's capital and reduced the inhabitants to slavery. We find for instance in an inscription a Pândiyan king of Madura exulting in the fact that he had demolished the whole of the city of Tanjore and ploughed up the area covered with the dwellings of the poor. A Chola king calls himself in revenge the "death of Madura." When the Muhammadans seized Devagiri, a century or so later, they captured the gallant Hindu prince of that country and flayed him alive. Ferishta, the historian of the Dakhan, gives us an idea of what war meant in the days of Muhammad Shâh Bahmani and the Râjah of Vijayanagar. When the Sultan took Adoni he slew, after the battle, 70,000 innocent country-folk, men, women and children. After another great battle, the Muhammadan historian himself relates that the king "gave orders to resume the massacre of the unbelievers. They were executed with such strictness that pregnant women and even children at the breast, did not escape the sword." At the pursuit of the Râjah by the Sultan up to the walls of Vijayanagar, Ferishta says "that 10,000 of the enemy were slain, but this did not satisfy the rage of the Sultan, who commanded the inhabitants of every place round Beejanugger to be massacred without mercy." The city was a very large one, and the suburbs very extensive, so that the slaughter of these helpless citizens must have been terrific. The Hindus told their king that 10,000 Brahmans alone had been killed in that awful holocaust.

At the great battle of Talikota, which settled the fate of the last Hindu sovereignty in Southern India, the Muhammadan allies slaughtered 100,000 of their foes; and immediately afterwards the magnificent city of Vijayanagar, falling into the hands of the victors, was reduced to ashes. It had been, as I have stated, a city of vast size, the outer walls measuring 28 miles round, and beyond these were many suburban towns and villages. The whole of the citizens were slaughtered or driven out, and their houses plundered. Ferishta admits that his co-religionists on this occasion "committed all manner of excess." He adds that the "depredations of the allies destroyed all the country round," and that the city was so devastated that it became a heap of ruins totally uninhabited. It remains so to this day, save for the peaceful villages that have sprung up in the midst of the magnificent vegetation and smiling rice fields that now occupy the spot where once stood the palaces and streets of the old capital.

A little later our author describes the successful attack on a fortress, and writes: "The soldiers . . . . . . put to death indiscriminately the noble, the rich, the master and the servant, the merchant, the pilgrim, and the travelling stranger. Their houses were set on fire. . . . Virgins whose modesty concealed their faces from the sun and moon were dragged by the hair into the assemblies of the drunken."

Such was war and such were the sufferings of innocent citizens in the days of Muhammadan supremacy, and the fighting, carnage and rapine lasted till the days of the English conquest. The people suffered endless misery, which, as well stated by Mr. Srînivasa Râghavaiyangâr, "was borne with patience and resignation as they had no experience of a happier condition."

In the middle of the 16th century marauders were so numerous (*op. cit.* p. 3) that a traveller by night was almost certain to fall into their hands. Father Martin in the 18th century says that the Kallar tribes of the Madura district were "more barbarous than any savages in any part of the globe." Thugs infested the country and murdered helpless travellers wholesale. There were no roads. Tavernier, in the middle of the 17th century, found that wheeled carriages could not journey between Masulipatam, the then flourishing seaport, and Golconda, the nearest capital (*id.*, p. 16). It was with great difficulty that he managed to get a small cart to Golconda, and he was obliged to take it to pieces in several places and carry them. And from Golconda all the way south to Cape Comorin there were no wagons at all. Oxen and pack-horses were used for conveying merchandise. Burhânpur is described as a ruined town. At Sironj there existed a band of artizans who made muslins of exquisite fineness, but "the merchants were not allowed to export them, and the Governor sent them *all* for the use of the Great Mogul's seraglio and of the principal courtiers." Patna was one of the largest towns in India, but the houses were nearly all roofed with thatch or bamboo. Dacca was a town of miserable huts made of bamboo and mud. Merchants were frequently plundered by the râjahs of the territories through which they had to pass The dispensation of justice was very summary and unencumbered with forms. There were no jails, for the custom of the country was not to keep men in prison. Tavernier visited a Navâb in the Cuddapah country, and saw a trial of some criminals. One had his hands and feet cut off and was thrown into a field by the roadside to end his days. Another had his stomach slit open and was flung into a drain. The others were decapitated. He continues: "The peasants have for their sole garment a scrap of cloth tied round their loins, and are reduced to great poverty, because, if the governors become aware that they possess any property they seize it straightway. . . . . You may see in India whole provinces like deserts, from whence the peasants have fled on account of the oppression of the governors." The Chingleput

District was almost entirely depopulated by the wars with Haidar Ali of Mysore. So much so that "hardly any other signs were left in many parts of the country of its having been inhabited than the bones of the bodies that had been massacred, or the naked walls of the houses, choultries and temples which had been burnt ("*Fifth Report*," *op. cit.*, p. 20). And yet Mr. Schwartz, a missionary, wrote that the people of Tanjore, then in the possession of the Nawâb of Arcot, would even "have preferred Hyder's invasion to the Nawab's occupation," so terrible were their sufferings. Though cultivation was so much restricted, the Nâwab extorted from the landholders as much as double the present land-revenue of the district. In the Zamindâr and Poligâr countries the only limit to the exaction was the ryot's ability to pay. Where there were no Zamindârs, renters were placed in charge of villages, and mercilessly fleeced the people. Sir Thomas Munro, writing of the condition of the Ceded Districts at the beginning of the century, states that the numerous petty chiefs (they were about 80 in number) employed 30,000 armed men in gangs to force the so-called rents and taxes out of the people. And the best proof of this miserable condition of the country is that to this day the villages of that tract and the lower Dakhan are all walled fortresses with a watch-tower in the centre to which the unhappy cultivators fled for safety against their oppressors and the gangs of marauders who were wont to attack them. Buchanan describes this state of things in 1800 A.D. and writes: "The country has been in a constant state of warfare and the poor inhabitants have suffered too much from all parties to trust in any."

In Trichinopoly according to the Collector, Mr. Wallace, in 1802 the condition of the ryots had been that of abject slavery. The grain raised was an absolute State monopoly of the Nawâb's, so much so that if a ryot lent another a small quantity of grain even for personal consumption he was severely fined.

Tippoo Sultan, when he paid his soldiers, was wont temporarily to fix an arbitrary enhanced value on his coins so that the men obtained from the merchants a greater quantity of produce than was due, the value being again lowered after a few weeks.

The realization of revenue by means of torture was one of the recognised institutions of the country. In 1855 there was a Commission in Madras for the investigation of the system of tortures constantly resorted to in the villages for the collection of revenue, and long lists are given in their Report of cruelties habitually practised.*

---

* A recent writer to a London paper (Mr. H. P. Malet in the "*Morning Post*") states that when he was in Sholapur in 1832 he found the ryots so preyed upon by the money-lenders that they were paying, or trying to pay, interest on loans at a rate settled on the system of payment in kind for advances of grain, that actually

These instances might be amplified to almost any extent, but I will abandon this branch of the subject with the remark that it concerns all classes, not merely the agriculturists. All that I desire to insist on is that the people of India ought to be taught the truth; so long as they remain in ignorance they will cherish the belief that in days before the English the people were better off and happier than they are now.

FAMINES.

It is an entire mistake to suppose that famines have only taken place of late years, or that in any way British administration is responsible for their recurrence. They have occurred in all ages, and in former times the people were infinitely worse off. They had no resources wherewith to meet the scarcity, and their rulers took little or no pains to save life. Even so far back as the date of the *Râmâyana* we read of severe and prolonged drought in Upper India. According to Orissa legends there were terrible famines early in the twelfth century A.D. South India preserves a memory of a famine many years ago that lasted for twelve years, at the end of which the whole country was desolate and depopulated. It is supposed to have occurred in A.D. 1396. Ferishta mentions two disastrous famines in the 15th century, of which the latter was the worst. The whole of middle India from sea to sea became a barren waste, and very large numbers died of starvation. When the rain at last came there were hardly any farmers left to till the ground. In 1570 there was a terrible famine on the west coast. In 1648 in the Coimbatore country, a great part of the population died. In 1659 there was another, and in one small tract, amongst the Christians alone, upwards of 10,000 perished miserably. In 1677 there was famine in Madura. In 1709 there was a very prolonged drought of several years' duration. In 1733 there was a famine in the Chingleput district. In 1780 one over the whole of the Carnatic. From 1789 to 1792 there was a terrible famine in the Northern Sarkârs, and the people died in thousands

---

amounted, on careful examination, to 300 per cent. It was "2½ seers at harvest time to 1 seer at seed time." Interest on money loans at the same time was "100 to 150 per cent. compound." "Many ryots had bound themselves over on scraps of paper......for service to the creditor for a certain number of years, or for life...... ordinary debtors were liable to various kinds of torture." He confirms my remarks about roads. There were none in the District in those days. As to interest on loans the British Government has instituted a system of small agricultural loans by the State at a payment of 6 per cent. interest for the benefit of the farmers, while the British Courts of Justice flatly refuse to countenance the enormous demands of the creditors, and on suits by creditor against debtor decree payment at a moderate and reasonable rate. Slavery and torture have, of course, been abolished utterly. To our door is somtimes laid the poverty of the Indian labourer and small farmer, but I think it must be admitted that England has tried to assist him, while the native governments uniformly neglected his interests.

(*op. cit.*, pp. 4-8). If we knew more of the past history of India we should find that seasons of scanty rain-fall have perpetually recurred, as they are now recurring, in the natural order of things which man's will cannot alter.

But how was the distress met in pre-English days, and how is it met now? There is no need to recapitulate the provisions of the English Government for the purpose of saving life, and protecting and preserving those in difficulty and distress. In Sir Charles Elliot's able paper on the subject recently read before the Society of Arts in London, will be found an epitome of the whole scheme. It is not too much to say that in days of Hindu and Muhammadan administration little or *nothing* was done. The rulers apparently saw no necessity for attempting to save life, and left the people to themselves; and that this spirit even now survives may be gathered from an extract which I append from a telegram sent from Agra by a Special Famine Correspondent to the "*Morning Post*" on February 18th of this year. "Since last telegraphing, I have inspected the central Native States and the Bundalkhand District. In the native states the authorities have been extremely supine, and no relief has been provided. The people consequently are flocking into British territory. . . . The villagers, themselves practically destitute, are turning the mendicants away, and many are dying on the railway line, succumbing in their efforts to walk from one station to another."

Let this be compared with English energy, sympathy, and commiseration; with the fact that several English officers have died at their post, struggling to help the people of the country; and with the magnificent contributions sent out from England in 1877, and in the present year, for the relief of the poor and suffering.

Roads and Communications, etc.

Very little time need be spent in considering the change brought about in the freedom of the Hindu villager by the immense road and railway works carried out under British administration. Railways of course there were none in old days. At present their construction is proceeding with great rapidity. As to roads, I will contrast the past and present only in my own District, Bellary, which will serve as an example of what has been done all over India. Prior to our taking over the country there was not one mile of made road in all the length and breadth of the district, and only very few tracks from place to place, half the district being composed of what we term "black-cotton soil"—an alluvial deposit impassable in wet weather. At the present day there are 1,000 miles of road maintained by the Local Board. They are, I am bound to say, not all of them in very sound travelling condition during the rains, but the good work is progressing; and remember that villagers can travel at night from end to end of the District without being, as was the case in former days, in hourly danger of murder by Thugs. There has been no thuggee in the country for the last sixty years. Some few petty dacoities there are, but it may be said that travellers there by night are almost as safe as in England, and in the day-time quite as safe. The trouble from bands of thieves is confined to a very small area, and the thieves themselves as a rule do not use violence, they only seek to terrify. This entire absence of the means of travel in former days is a point I am anxious to press, because I think it is not sufficiently grasped by the modern Hindu. When I have ventured to mention the fact —an historic fact—to Hindu gentlemen in India it has been received in a spirit of entire incredulity, and this even amongst my highly-educated, well-informed and most trusted Hindu officials, whose loyalty to the Crown is unquestionable. I could never persuade them of the truth. And my want of success in this direction forms part of the basis upon which rests my conviction that historical ignorance is far more wide-spread than we often think, and that it is becoming, if not a positive political danger, at least a matter for very deep regret.

Some other British Improvements.

Let me, before concluding, very briefly point out how the condition of the villager of to-day has been benefited by English administration.

I have already alluded to the immense reduction in the amount of taxation and the sweeping away of scores of harassing and inquisitorial imposts; to the present simple and regular mode of collection of the land-revenue, with regard to which every farmer knows the exact amount due, and need never pay a farthing more; to the great reduction effected therein; to the raising of the people from a condition of slavery to one of an independence and freedom not exceeded by that of any dweller in this land of England; to the network of roads and communications now established throughout the country, and the abolition of thuggee and dacoitee, which enable a villager, formerly confined absolutely to his own village and unable to trade, to travel freely from end to end of the country, and embark in merchandise to the extent of his capabilities with every nation in the world. Let me now note some few minor points.

We have established an Imperial Postal system over all India, even in small villages. It will doubtless perfect itself by degrees, but I remember only 28 years ago when I was first sent "up-country" that there was in existence an institution called the "District Tappal," the Imperial system not being at that time so fully developed as it is now, and that the so-called "runners" would sometimes take three weeks or a month to convey letters to a distance of forty miles. Prior to the assumption of Government by the English there had been no regular postal system at all. Hospitals have been and are being constructed all over India, and dispensaries have been multiplied, so that the unfortunate victim of accident need never be left, as formerly, with his wounds or broken limbs untended, or badly treated by uneducated quacks.

Schools, too, are everywhere multiplying and primary education is being rapidly extended, with the result that the farmers are in a better position than before to protect themselves against the extortion of grasping village officers, and all classes of the community are aided in matters of daily trade.

I will only make a passing reference to the fact that England has provided India with a set of officials whose single aim from morning till night is, in spite of all opposition and in the face of all difficulties, to do the right; to protect the persons and property, and secure the welfare of every individual resident in the country.

As to the charge that we have pauperized the country I leave that to experts, merely remarking that in a few years of my experience between 1868 and 1894 I saw everywhere villages improving, brick and tiled houses being substituted for mud huts with thatched roofs, though of course it cannot be denied that the latter are still in the majority; I saw towns becoming enlarged, and fine houses being built; I saw drainage and general sanitation attempted; I found wages rising, and rise of wages is a sure sign of prosperity and wealth; I observed a growing independence and self-reliance in classes of the community formerly oppressed and down-trodden; I watched a constant growth of litigation, and though this is of course to be deprecated, still it implies an increase of wealth in the litigious classes. Population also has enormously increased in the last century, and this is always accepted as a test of the improving condition of the masses. I may of course be entirely wrong, but in a hundred ways I have seemed to see the country improving; and am convinced that the last century of British administration has resulted generally in the conferring of enormous benefits on the bulk of the people of India.*

With this view it is a source of constant pain to me to think that even the well-educated section of the Hindu community do

* I do not deny that certain classes are not so well off as they used to be. The families of Rájahs, large landowners, experienced artizans, have doubtless suffered. The Brahman element, the intellect and mind of India, though it has greater scope for general education, has less for the exercise of local influence, and here is where the pinch is most greatly felt. With every sympathy for these gentlemen, I cannot blind my eyes to what England has done for the masses.

not recognise what we have done for the people of India, and are so loud in their assertion that we have done, and are doing, harm. It seems to me that this outcry can only arise from a deep-seated ignorance of the facts of history which prevents them from forming a just comparison between the Past and the Present. I venture, therefore, to plead for an extension of sound historical education in India. History ought to be taught in all schools and colleges—not merely lists of dates and leading events, and names of kings,—but such history as will enable the Hindus to obtain a true insight into the condition of their country in past ages, and afford them a means by which they may estimate aright the change wrought during the years of British administration—whether that change be for better or worse. At present I think that they have no conception at all of what that change has been.